W9-ANG-704

THIS BOOK BELONGS TO:

Your Brightest Life

JOURNAL

A CREATIVE GUIDE TO BECOMING YOUR BEST SELF

Caroline Kelso Zook

CHRONICLE BOOKS
SAN FRANCISCO

Your brightest, most satisfying life rests in figuring out who you are and what you want—and then courageously acting on those truths in all that you do.

ISBN: 978-1-4521-7019-0

Manufactured in China.

MIX
Paper from
responsible sources
FSC™ C008047

10 9 8 7 6 5 4 3 2 1

Chronicle Books LLC
680 Second Street
San Francisco, California 94107
www.chroniclebooks.com

Contents

Welcome to Your Brightest Life

I like to imagine that we all arrived here on Earth as these bright little balls of colorful energy, full of nothing but pure potential.

I imagine each of us with a mix of colors, near electric in their brightness.

Encapsulated in these spirits is a one-of-a-kind mixture of talents, personality, thoughtfulness, strengths, likes, and desires—and no one else on Earth has the very same combination.

Maybe it's the artist in me, but this colorful collective is how I like to envision humanity.

Unfortunately, these orbs of pure potential don't stay this bright for long. Life happens. The messy work of being human takes over. Responsibilities, expectations, challenges, stress, financial pressures . . . they all manifest as veils of gray that start to dim our radiant, pure light. Under their weight, we compromise and settle and often reject our true selves in an effort to fit in. And in doing so, we get further from our original vibrance. The years go by, and we begin to lose that electric color that we began with.

My mission is to give you the tools to find your way back to your brightest, purest self. To reconnect with that essence of vibrant color and pure potential. And then to make choices each day that allow that essence to thrive.

That is the path of your brightest life.

This grand journey requires a great deal of unlearning and relearning. In order to find our way back to our truest selves, we have to get curious about what lies deep within us. We have to peel back the layers of the person we've become in order to get back down to the raw materials. Once we uncover those core components, then we can effectively reassemble ourselves again from the ground up, making sure to honor the parts of us that feel most essential to who we are.

I can speak so confidently about this theory of mine only because I've seen it play out in my own life. Growing up, I was your textbook overachiever. I was a people pleaser, and as a kid I learned that the best way to get the validation I so craved was to do well in school. My quest for academic achievement defined my entire adolescence.

At that time, the rules of life appeared to be so clear to me. You do well in school . . . you get a good job . . . you make good money . . . you are successful and happy. It seemed that simple.

But, as the years went by, first in high school and then in college, the more I focused my energy and attention on fitting in to this traditional model of success, the more I felt this nagging voice inside begging me to alter my path.

This knowing voice would send me tiny reminders about how I'd actually been a really creative kid. I would flash back to memories of my youth, when I was full of ideas and always found excuses to make things with my hands. Our kitchen table was often covered with the remnants of one project or another.

Despite the immense joy these activities brought me, it never once dawned on me that being an artist was a viable or acceptable path in life. The signals I got from teachers and my parents seemed to convey that creativity should be relegated to hobbies or side projects, and couldn't compare to the implied prestige of a job or, even better, a "career."

These messages taught me to suppress my creative impulses in favor of things that would get me closer to the model of success I thought I should aspire to.

That is until college, when I got really clever and thought I'd cracked the code on combining these two seemingly opposing forces. I thought I could have the best of both worlds by pursuing a career in advertising—a creative industry with real "career potential."

I quickly realized that this combination didn't actually appease my ongoing inner conflict; it only made it worse. Starting a career in a "creative field" so painfully devoid of creativity as I knew it (the freedom, the sense of play, the unlimited possibilities) only made me more aware of my deep desire to experience the joy of making things again. I didn't want deadlines and spreadsheets and client negotiations. I wanted self-expression and discovery and beauty.

It didn't take me long to realize I had to get out of there. I had people around me telling me, *Don't worry, it's normal. No one likes their first job.* Or my favorite, *Everyone has to pay their dues the first ten years, then you can make your own hours and call the shots.*

What?! A decade of misery for an uncertain future when

I *maybe* could have the freedom to create what I wanted to create? That felt like a terrible plan to me. Every day I spent at a job I hated, I felt as if that colorful core inside me was getting dimmer and quieter and nearly imperceptible. I knew I had to save her.

So I quit my job.

I didn't know it then, but that decision was the first bold step toward living my own brightest life.

It was my way of taking ownership of this pure, vibrant potential I've been given, and deciding to navigate my choices based on what would make my core self burn brighter, rather than letting it flicker out.

Once I experienced the pure freedom that comes from building a life where I get to be the brightest version of myself, it became a feeling I wanted to seek out over and over again. It felt as if I were a bird trapped in a cage within cages, and every time I unlocked a new door I experienced an expanded sense of freedom.

I began writing about my experiences on a personal blog as a way to lean into the creativity I was finally waking up to. As I gained confidence and began to embrace this truer version of myself (not the one interested in being "successful," but the one interested in being *authentic*), more people became attracted to my writing.

Then the big leap came in 2014, when I decided to make this creative endeavor my full-time occupation. That year, I started my business, Made Vibrant, a design studio and blog dedicated to exploring the intersection of creativity, personal growth, and authentic business. Every day, I was getting more curious about who I really was, and I wanted to share that journey with others. I was starting to understand that values like creativity and flexibility and self-discovery were integral to my spirit, and starting my own business was my way of designing a life around those values and allowing my unique spirit to thrive.

It hasn't been an easy journey. I've had to break down every notion I grew up with about what success is or what a person *should* be, and I've had to relearn those things using my own inner wisdom instead.

Now I can happily say I'm cultivating a life that feels full of joy and freedom and full-on, technicolor self-expression. It's not a *perfect* life, but it's vibrant and feels connected to that pure place of colorful possibility within me.

That is what I want for you, too.

I want you to feel the overwhelming happiness that comes from living a life where your inner brightness can shine fully and unapologetically.

I want you to peel back the layers of gray that may have dimmed your bright potential, and shed them until you're left with nothing but pure, unbridled vibrance.

I want you to develop the confidence to unleash your creativity and share it with the world.

I want you to unearth the courage within you to stand firm in your authenticity even if it means risking rejection.

Because that's what *Your Brightest Life Journal* is all about.

How to Use This Journal

First off, do me a favor, would you? Please don't be afraid of this book! I used to be one of those people who would buy a beautiful new notebook or journal and be so afraid of "messing it up" that it sat unused, collecting dust on my shelf.

That's not what I want for this book (or for you)! The guidance in this journal is useful only if you **use it** (obviously)—so please do! I want you to write in it, draw in it, scribble in the margins, rough it up, and run it ragged.

In fact, to get over the fear of "messing it up" right away, let's start with a little challenge. I want you to scribble in this little box right here. Don't you dare try to make it pretty! Just give yourself permission to put pen (or marker or paint or whatever you have nearby) to paper and see what comes out. Consider it your first act of creative courage in this journal.

Did you do it? See . . . that was kind of fun, right? Now the seal has been broken! You have officially given yourself permission to create freely in the pages that follow. Hold on to that feeling!

This book will take you on a journey through seven sections, each one presenting an essential step in the quest to forging your brightest life. You can read them in sequence or you can turn to the appropriate section whenever you need some encouragement during a particular time in your life.

You'll notice there are four types of pages in this journal. Each one has a different purpose and can be used in different ways:

ART PAGES

Throughout this journal there are more than sixty vibrant hand-lettered phrases and nuggets of wisdom that have helped me stay mindful of my brightest life. Don't be afraid to tear these out and hang them in your home or office to serve as messages of encouragement to bring you back to your own inner wisdom.

STORIES

Each section begins with a bit of context, sharing parts of my own personal journey to my brightest life and the advice that has helped me live more colorfully and authentically.

GET CREATIVE EXERCISES

Bust out the markers, pens, and crayons, because we're about to get interactive! The creative exercises are tasks where I'll ask you to fill in, write, color, or otherwise create, so that you can uncover new insights about yourself while visualizing the concepts I share within the journal.

FREE WRITE PROMPTS

Finally, you'll find good old-fashioned lined pages with simple journal prompts inviting you to write down your thoughts and feelings. Navigating your way back to your brightest self is about asking the right questions, and these pages will encourage you to get some clarity about what's in that heart of yours.

Join the Conversation

This journal is the guide I wish I'd had when I was finding my way to my brightest life. I hope you feel every ounce of love I poured into these pages.

To join the conversation and read more about what I believe it takes to live your brightest life, you can head to my blog at MadeVibrant.com or hang out with the incredible community of soulful creatives over on my Instagram (@ckelso). I'd absolutely love it if you'd share your journey with me by posting photos of your work in this journal using the tag #brightestlifejournal and tagging me (@ckelso). Nothing makes me happier than seeing others striving toward their brightest life.

I sincerely believe the world is a better place when we all show up as our best, brightest selves.

My hope is that you'll use this journal to figure out exactly what that means for you. Now let's get started!

SECTION 1
Self-Awareness

The greatest thing you'll ever endeavor to study is yourself.

FIND out WHO you REALLY are.

In order to live your brightest, most vibrant life, you first have to be honest with yourself about who you are at the deepest level and what is important to you.

The exercises in this section are focused on introducing you to your truest inner self and all the things that make you unique. It's important to recognize your natural strengths and gifts, define your core values, and appreciate the unique combination of talents, traits, and passions that is central to your identity in order to move toward a life and career that honors your true potential.

"Who am I?" It's a daunting question, isn't it?

It feels infinite and unsettlingly powerful. It's a question so big that, in response, many of us resort to rattling off nouns that define us in relation to the work we do or the people we care for or the things we like. *I'm a daughter, a business owner, a coffee lover . . .*

But these are not really identifying qualities that set us apart from the other seven billion people on Earth. In fact, they're the opposite; they're opportunities for us to prove we're a part of the herd. *Oh, you're a daughter, too? How great that you also have a successful career! You like coffee, too?*

And this desire we have (the instinct to define ourselves in a way that makes us feel *together* rather than *separate*) is at the heart of what's holding so many of us back from our truest potential.

I know from experience.

When I was a freshman in college, I wanted to be a doctor. (Or, rather, I *thought* I wanted to be a doctor.) Going to medical school sounded impressive and prestigious, like something my parents would love to gush about with their friends.

The only problem? I'm completely squeamish, extremely sensitive, and frankly, very uncomfortable making split-second decisions. Not exactly a recipe for an effective medical professional.

It took me several semesters before I questioned where this "dream" of mine was coming from. Was it a dream that was coming from *inside me* or *outside me?*

In other words, was it stemming from my deepest core self, or was it a dream I thought I *should* dream because it would bring me validation from the people around me?

When I got quiet with myself, I remembered I had always been a deeply creative kid. My hands perpetually covered in paint, art supplies strewn across the living room floor, staying up all hours of the night to perfect my school project diorama—these memories seemed most closely tied to who I actually felt I was.

I am a maker. I am a dreamer. I am a feeler.

Once I followed the tiny bread crumbs back to that truer, deeper part of myself, I felt a new wholeness in my heart. This was a signal my soul was sending me because it could sense I was getting closer to uncovering my true self. It made me wonder what other signals my true inner self had been sending me that I'd just been too busy or blind to pay attention to.

Part one of my process of self-discovery was unlearning the stories about my identity that had been built on this idea of what I was *supposed* to want. But part two was developing a language between my head and my heart so that I could wake up to what I truly wanted instead.

That pit in the bottom of my stomach? I learned that usually means I'm headed down a path that doesn't quite jive with who I am, and even if I know what I have to do, I'm dreading the hard conversation I need to have with myself in order to course-correct.

But that feeling of floating and ease that sometimes washes over me? That's usually a strong indicator that I'm making time for my self-expression, and I'm sharing my truth courageously with others.

This is the vocabulary I've developed with myself over time, an awareness that allows me to tap into those whispers that sit at the bottom of my soul. Getting my conscious self (my head) to speak the language of my unconscious self (my heart) was the missing piece that helped lead me back to my brightest core self.

Now I want to teach you how to do the same.

I want you to listen to what those whispers at the bottom of your soul are trying to tell you. I want you to forge a connection between your head and your heart so you know when your soul is thriving, and when it's being diminished. I want you to become so confident and clear on what makes you tick, that you know exactly how to return to yourself when life inevitably throws you its crazy curveballs.

Now I want to offer up that expansive, truth-bearing question to you again:

Who are YOU? Who are you *really* at your deepest core level?

It's okay if you don't know the answer right now, because the exercises and prompts in this section are designed to help you uncover just that.

You already have the answer to who you really are within you. Now it's time to peel back the layers of who you've been *trying* to be, the dreams you've thought you *should* have, and the people you've been trying to please, in order to reveal the truth of what's underneath.

Let's begin.

FreeDom feels like...

When do you feel like your freest self? What experiences, activities, decisions, and values make your spirit feel expansive?

What makes you come Alive?

THE many Layers of...

Picture yourself as a gobstopper (because it's a lot tastier than picturing yourself as an onion). Now fill out the layers below with the parts of yourself that show up for others and the parts that feel most essential to your core. Get creative decorating your gobstopper with a design that feels representative of your unique spirit and experience.

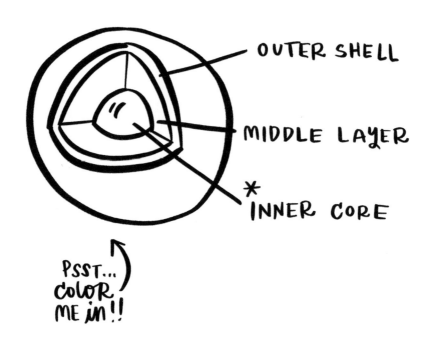

OUTER SHELL

MIDDLE LAYER

* INNER CORE

PSST... COLOR ME in!!

OUTER SHELL

What are qualities most people know about you? What are
the most visible ways that you show up in the world?

MIDDLE LAYER

What are things your close friends know about you?
What takes a little longer to get to know about you?

INNER CORE

What qualities feel most central to your identity? How would you
describe yourself if no one else was here to hear it?

Embracing your INNeR Black SHeeP

A funny thing happens when you share the facets of yourself you're most afraid to show—you're suddenly able to step in to that part of yourself that naturally strays from the herd. Maybe it's that you're irreverent or idealistic or critical or nerdy or a worrier or quiet—these hidden, unique traits may make you feel different, but they also hold the key to truly *connecting* in order to feel understood. I call these your "black sheep" qualities, and they are a part of the authentic YOU.

Write down some of your own black sheep qualities and try reframing them in a positive way. How do they make you YOU? What are some small ways that you can start letting these qualities shine through in your daily life? How can you embrace them and let others see them more freely?

your Light-up list

What lights you up? Think about where your curiosity has led you in the past. When do you feel happiest? What's something you've always loved to do? What activities and experiences are you most drawn to? Write down as many of these activities, interests, and experiences as you can. Draw these as various light sources to remind yourself to follow their shine: a sun, star, lantern, spotlight, and so on.

messages from your CORE

It's important to be able to recognize when your core self is telling you to move forward or pull back. This takes some understanding of how your intuition is trying to communicate with you. Use this page to fill in some physical and emotional signals your intuition uses to let you know when your soul is feeling freed or stifled. Be sure to include cues from both positive situations and negative situations so that the next time you make a decision, you'll know what sensations to be aware of when you "go with your gut." Think of it like a conversation between your head and your heart.

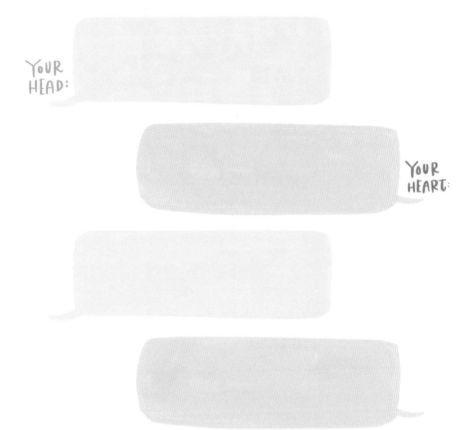

YOUR
HEAD:

YOUR
HEART:

clues FROM YOUR INNER KID

Memories from our past can sometimes hold clues to parts of ourselves we've suppressed as adults. What are some interests you had as a kid? What did you spend most of your time doing? When did the hours seem to fly by? Are there ways you can take some of those clues and infuse them into your adult life?

Pay ATTENTION to what Draws You IN

YOU
READY
ALREADY
KNOW
THE
ANSWER

Connect the Dots

There is buried treasure hidden in the connections between things that appear to be separate. Next to each dot, write a different interest, passion, or curiosity that you have. Then, on the connecting lines, write down the themes that link each pair. Look for patterns in these connections and celebrate the new treasures you've uncovered!

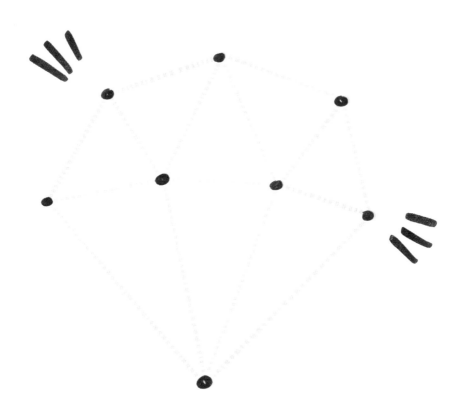

Story of your Life

Imagine your life as a book. What would the major chapters be? What about the plot twists that brought about big change? Use the book outline below to map your own life story.

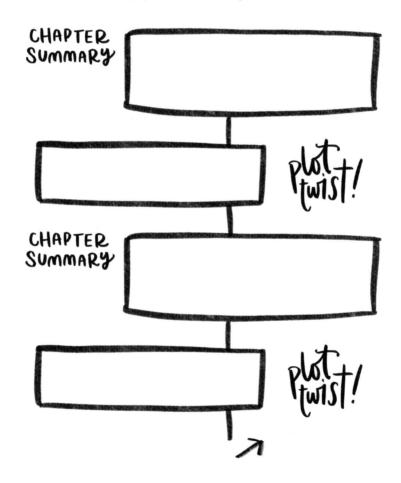

CHAPTER SUMMARY

plot twist!

CHAPTER SUMMARY

plot twist!

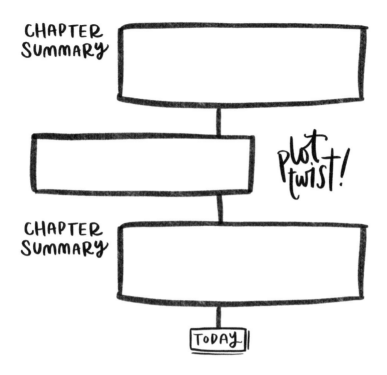

CHAPTER SUMMARY

plot twist!

CHAPTER SUMMARY

TODAY

Now, look back through each chapter of your life for patterns. What values motivated your progress? How have you evolved over time? What have you found yourself drawn to again and again?

Fuel for your Soul

Energy is one of the best tools in our self-awareness toolbox. When we feel energized, we're able to more clearly engage in a dialogue with our emotions, and we're more likely to set intentions to live out our values. But first, we need to get clear on what brings us energy and what drains us. What's one activity that you continue to engage in that you know drains you? What's one activity that charges you up but that you don't make enough time for right now? What areas of your life benefit when you're energized?

YOUR imPerfections are what make you Beautiful

Clarifying Your Core Values

You may have a good idea of what personality traits make you who you are, but there's nothing quite as revealing as what you care about and what drives your decisions. This exercise is all about defining your core values—those things that are most important to you. Scan the list below and color in the words that resonate with the values close to your heart! If you don't see one of your core values listed, use the empty lines to write them in!

adventure CALm community control
creativity joy curiosity contribution
compassion diversity discipline
efficiency empathy enthusiasm excellence
freedom faith generosity family health
fitness honesty fun growth
independence honor intuition justice
leadership legacy love loyalty
mastery openness positivity practicality
reliability sensitivity service simplicity
strength tolerance trust vitality

_____ _____ _____ _____

Now it's time to prioritize! Not sure which values are MOST important to you? Use the space below to compare two values at a time so you know which ones are most essential to who you are.

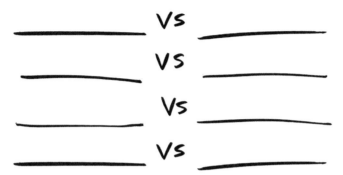

Finally, write your top five values in order of importance to you (at this moment in your life). This will help you remember what is vital to your truest self, and you can come back to this list anytime you want to make a decision aligned with those core values.

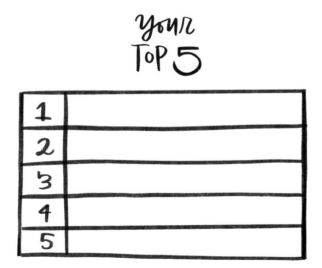

SECTION 2

AuTHENTiciTY

PLAY by your own RULES.

Simply put, authenticity is aligning
what you do with who you are.

In other words, it's making sure your actions reflect and honor the truest parts of yourself.

Remember that bright ball of pure potential that I talked about in the introduction? Authenticity is about making decisions that allow that energy to shine.

When your actions are out of alignment with who you are at your core, there's a dissonance you can sense in your soul. That tiny voice will whisper to you, *This isn't what's right for us.*

By contrast, when your actions are in alignment with your core being, there's an ease and a flow that you can sense as well. That tiny voice will whisper, *This feels amazing! More of this, please!*

I like to call this little voice your "Core Compass"—the gentle nudge of your heart that is always trying to point you to your True North.

Once you're able to unearth what makes you unique at the most essential level—what you like, what you value, what you gravitate toward, what makes you feel free, what you desire—that is when you will carry the most powerful decision-making tool you've ever known. Your Core Compass will continue to point you toward your most authentic path.

Now, sure, all of that is great in theory, but let's get real. If authentic living is so simple, why does it feel so complicated? Why does it feel so hard sometimes to make decisions if all we have to do is follow the voice of our authentic selves?

Well, mostly it's due to that little inconvenient fact that we don't exist on this planet alone. Our decisions are interconnected with so many people surrounding us—our family and friends on the small scale, as well as society and the culture at large.

Despite the fact that our hearts wish to feel free and fully expressed, they also want to feel accepted and loved. We're sent all kinds of messages from the people around us about what's expected of us, and our fear is that if we make a different choice (a more authentic choice), we will be rejected or ridiculed.

These cues about what is expected, what our responsibilities are, what is considered normal or practical—these are powerful forces that can often interfere with the magnetism of our Core Compass.

That's when it's crucial to make space away from the hustle and bustle of daily life so that we can tune in to that pure voice inside that helps us discern whether we want something because we really want it, or if we want it because we think we're supposed to want it.

Over the years, I've gotten better at separating these two things. For instance, a few years ago my husband, Jason, and I were living in Florida. We owned a house, both of our families lived in the same city with us, and for a time we thought we'd probably stay there forever. That was until we could both feel a desire bubbling up in us to experience new things and get out of our comfort zones. Adventure, growth, and discovery were all values that felt central to our core selves, yet our life-style decisions weren't reflecting those values. We wanted to move, but we kept convincing ourselves to stay. *We can't*, we'd say. *We should stay here with our families. We should wait until the market is better to sell our house.* Should, should, should. (It was a real should-show!)

Finally we got fed up with waking up every day to a life we knew wasn't really honoring our true desire for adventure and growth. So we decided to sell most of our belongings, pack up our car, and move to California.

That decision felt hard in the moment because others' expectations were clouding our judgment. But once we were able to tune in to what we really wanted, it was actually an easy decision to make.

Living authentically means questioning conventions and expectations. When you find yourself saying *I can't . . .* or *I shouldn't . . .* challenge yourself to dig into those limiting beliefs. WHY can't you? WHY shouldn't you?

One question that I always find to be heart-expanding is this: **What if it doesn't have to be this way?**

You might find that a whole new world of possibilities opens up, once you suspend those shoulds and play out the scenario as if your true self is calling all the shots.

It's important to remember that you can choose to do things differently than everyone around you. The rules that you feel exist are just an illusion. When your vision for your life goes beyond the frame of "normal," you can choose to shatter the frame and build yourself a new one.

You *can* leave that job that's draining your spirit. You *can* make that move. Or chase that dream. You *can* quit that project that's no longer serving you.

Will it be comfortable? No. You will need to have hard conversations to get there.

But life's truly liberating decisions often involve temporary discomfort and hard conversations.

Remind yourself that on the other side of those things waits a life where you get to show up fully as your true self. When you do this, you allow yourself to be fully seen, and when you allow yourself to be fully seen, you allow yourself to be fully loved. There is no better feeling in the world.

Each of us is given one life to spend any way that we want. Don't let the fears or expectations of others tell you how to spend yours.

In all decisions, both big and small, ask yourself:

Does this decision or action honor who
I am and what I believe at my core?

If the answer is YES, you're on the path to your brightest life.

THE TASTE of your TRUTH

Authenticity is all about choosing freedom, but it's important to learn what that feels like on a cellular level so you know in your gut when you're taking action in alignment with your truth.

Think back to a time when you were confronted with a decision and you chose to remain true to yourself. What did it feel like? How did you know it was congruent with your core self? What were the signs your body, heart, and mind sent you to confirm your decision was stemming from your authenticity?

Authenticity is ALIGNING Who YOU ARe and WHaT YOU Do

Alignment IN Action

Authenticity is about aligning your actions (what you do) with your core being (who you are). It's about engaging in activities and making choices that support the deepest, truest parts of you: your beliefs, values, likes, and unique personality. To see this alignment in action, start by filling in the top circle with words and phrases that represent who you are. Then fill in the lower circle with actions you take, activities you engage in, and things you devote your time to in your life, career, relationships, and so on.

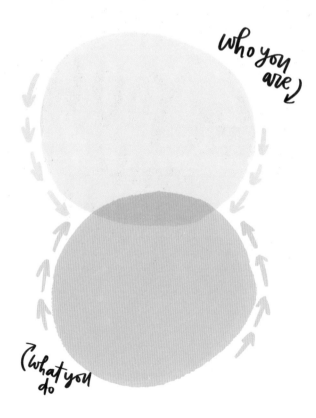

who you are)

(what you do

Now take stock. Do the circles feel aligned? Are you making choices and exhibiting behaviors that feel congruent with who you are at your core?

Fill in the overlapping circles below with all the activities and choices that feel completely aligned with who you are at your core so you can visualize that state of total authentic alignment.

when who you are
meets what you do

Shake OFF the SHOULDS

Releasing expectations

Part of living an authentic life requires us to let go of expectations we feel others have placed on us. It could be things our culture expects of us, our families expect of us, or our partners expect of us.

Are there times when you feel confined by what's expected of you? How have these expectations made it hard for you to pursue an authentic life? Write down some of the expectations you feel obligated to so you can identify how they may be holding you back from your brightest life.

your CoRe Compass

Your "Core Compass" is what I call that inner True North that your intuition will always point to if you learn to tap into it. Your core values will point you in the right direction, if you can learn to hush the voices of everyone around you and pay attention. But, like any compass, it's helpful only if you know how to read it. Pretend this is your own inner Core Compass. At the north point, write down ways that your intuition guides you in the right direction. At the south point, write down ways you feel your compass alerts you that you're heading in the wrong direction.

ex) I feel light & excited

ex) Knot IN the pit of my stomach

A TOTAL SHOULD-Show

Should can be a dangerous word, because it leads us to make decisions based on what we think other people want us to do or obligations we feel, rather than the true desires in our hearts. Can you think of some decisions you've made, big or small, because you felt you should, not because you truly wanted to?

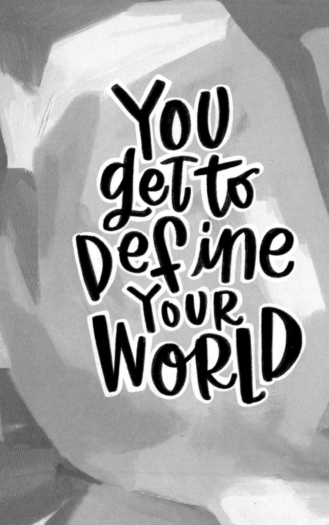

Authenticity Awards

Making choices in harmony with your core self is a reason to celebrate! Fill up the page below with badges, trophies, and ribbons for all the times you showed up honestly and vulnerably as your true self, even if you were afraid.

Living Beyond the Frame

I like to think of society's rules and expectations as a frame. Sometimes you have to break free of that frame in order to live your most vibrant, authentic life. To illustrate this, label pieces of the frame below with different boundaries placed on your life or expectations that make you feel confined. Now draw huge cracks in it to represent breaking the boundaries that are holding you back from the possibilities that exist beyond the frame.

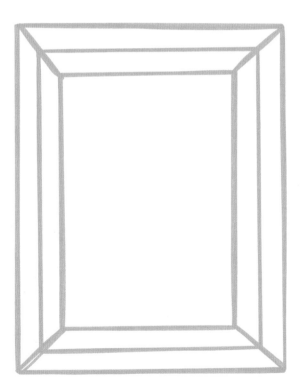

when the
FRame
DoeSn't
FIT,
SHatteR
THE
FRame

Practicing vulNerability

Do you feel you sometimes hold back who you truly are because you're afraid? Write down what these fears are and what you think might happen if you *did* allow yourself to be truly seen. Think of one small time or place in your life that you can show up more vulnerably and fully.

Freeing THE future

Planning out the future to a tee is one of the ways we get derailed from living our brightest life, because we fixate on a point in front of us rather than listening to what's inside of us. We focus so much on looking ahead that we forget to look within.

Use the space below to write down your plans and the things you've already defined as goals for your future. Then explain *why* you've set those goals. Is your motivation coming from a place of true desire, or what you think you *should* want? Finally, use the last column in the tables below to imagine different possibilities for each of those goals. Free up your future by becoming open to different outcomes.

Next month

the PLAN	WHY	WHAT if?

One Year from Now

the PLAN	WHY	WHAT if?

Five Years from Now

the PLAN	WHY	WHAT if?

Stop looking AHEAD and Start looking WITHIN.

ReWRiTiNg THE Rulebook

Living authentically means playing by your own rules, so it's time to write your own rulebook! Imagine that the rules and expectations you perceive can be rewritten in a way that allows you to show up as your truest, brightest self. What are those new rules? What can you give yourself permission to do or be? Issue yourself some directives and guidelines that can help you stay connected to this new life on your terms.

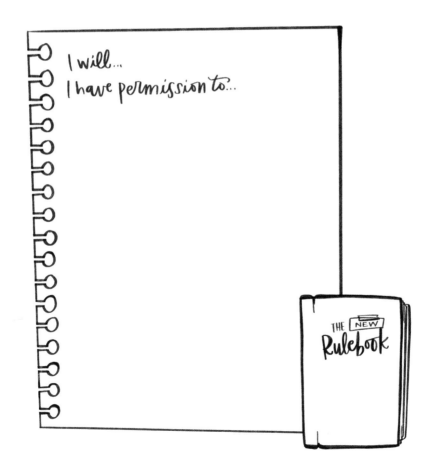

I will...
I have permission to...

THE NEW
Rulebook

SECTION 3
CReativity

CReativity
IS THE
Language
our Souls use
to communicate
with the WORLD.

Whatever's inside you begging to be EXPRESSED, free it.

Creativity is a beautiful instrument for self-discovery. The act of making asks us to trust our impulses, express ourselves freely, and turn our complex inner worlds into something that we can see or hear or touch and share with others.

This section is about encouraging you to find an outlet to continuously tap into that core part of you. It's about freeing the creativity that lives within you and encouraging artistic exploration. The pages that follow will help you follow the spark of curiosity, carve out intentional time for your creative practice, and find ways for you to develop your unique voice.

The most powerful and accessible way for me to tap into my intuition and come back to my authenticity is through my creative practice. That practice is always changing and evolving, but these days it includes painting, hand-lettering, illustrating, writing, and designing. However, these various disciplines weren't always a part of my daily life. They used to be merely dreams in my head and a longing in my heart.

While I was still working at the advertising job I despised right out of college, in idle moments I'd dream of a home art studio and hours spent listening to music while painting huge canvases. I thought of writing a book (like the one you're holding!) or illustrating children's books with colorful worlds of my own creation. I had always felt the pull toward these kinds of pursuits, but I spent years convincing myself that I wasn't creative *enough* to do things like that, that I didn't know what I was doing (as if anyone does!), so I didn't have permission to lean into that creativity.

For years, these dreams and desires sat dormant in my head. That is, until one day when that burden of untapped potential became too painful for me to keep inside. I felt I *had* to do something with all of my creative impulses—that I had to start living authentically by *taking action* in harmony with these desires that felt so essential to my spirit.

I had no idea what to create or how to share my creative ideas, so I did what felt most accessible and natural at the time: I started a blog. I was reluctant and full of doubt and, honestly, kind of embarrassed at first, wondering what my friends would think. Who did I think I was? Why did my voice matter? What did I have to say that was so important? The doubts continued to echo in my ear.

That is, until I hit "Publish" on my first post. That's when I experienced this sense of relief that's hard to describe. I felt lighter and freer, as though one of those gray veils had slowly lifted from my spirit.

I *made* something. I took those dreams and ideas in my head and I made them real. Words and thoughts that had existed in only the spaces of my mind were now available for others to read and connect with.

That feeling gave me an important revelation about my own creativity: that getting started wasn't really about *what* I had to share (or whether it was worth sharing); **the more important thing was that I was *sharing* it.**

It was the act of creating that my soul desperately wanted to engage in.

I truly believe all our untold stories and untapped potential turn into pockets of regret, which is a slippery slope leading to an entire *life* of regret.

Even if you have a hard time relating to the word *creative*, or (like me) if you've convinced yourself that you don't have whatever credentials are required to make what you want to make, let me assure you here in these pages, you ARE creative. You ARE qualified to make whatever your heart desires. We all are.

We are all perpetually making things. We make memories. We make noise. We make families. We make sandwiches. We make relationships, ideas, inventions, deductions . . . we're *making*-machines, constantly turning one thing into another.

Life itself is the ultimate act of creativity. We are all given this one vessel of potential, and the magic is in what we *make* of it.

So, leave your preconceptions at the door. Open yourself up to the self-discovery that can take place when you unleash what's inside you, begging to be expressed.

Mine the corners of your inner thoughts and experiences to bring forth the untold stories and creative gifts you have to share. Let yourself explore and play with a sense of childlike joy. Find a way to suspend judgment of your work for a while so that you have space to roam free until you find your unique creative voice. Don't be afraid to make a mistake or "mess up"—these imperfections are but interesting detours in the winding creative process.

Throughout this next section, lean into wonder, indulge your curiosity, and commit time to the creative process. Experience the freedom and satisfaction that comes with unleashing that inner brightness.

Collection of Curiosities

Even if you don't have a clear creative passion, sometimes all it takes is a tiny spark of curiosity to lead you to that means of self-expression that is so satisfying to your core self. Use the space below to draw different vessels and tiny trinkets representing things, recent or years old, that have piqued your curiosity (like that interesting mini-documentary on woodworking you saw, the music class you loved in middle school, or the friend who recently took up calligraphy). Then set a goal to revisit at least three of those activities in the coming month.

create for the
Joy
of it.

What MoveS me...

The feeling of being moved by something like a piece of art, an experience, or a conversation can be very powerful. That sensation is usually triggered by emotional resonance—a moment when an experience connects to a part of our core selves and we feel that connection in a deep way. Think of the last time you were creating something or you witnessed creativity and you felt moved. Describe that experience. What was it that moved you or resonated with you? What emotions came over you? What sensations did you feel?

exploring New territory

Label the land areas on this map with new directions and places you'd like to explore with your creativity, such as "Acrylic Paint Archipelago," "Short Story Land," "Ceramist Cove," and "The Strait of Spoken-Word Poetry." Use this map to conquer new territory, coloring in each area as you take steps in the next month to try out these hobbies or interests.

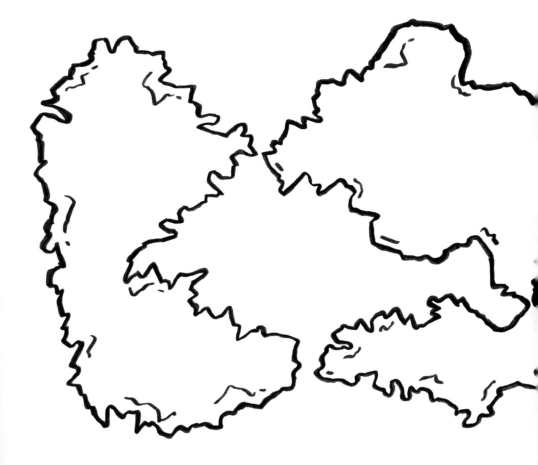

yes, I am CREATIVE.

We often carry preconceptions about what it means to be creative. These ideas and associations can stem all the way back to experiences we had as kids, or a time when we shared our creativity and felt rejected. Do you have any of these experiences that have affected the way you view your creativity? Use the space below to reaffirm your creativity and remind yourself of all the ways you are, in fact, creative.

CREATE
THAT THING
ONLY YOU
CAN CREATE

You Can't be AFRAID to MESS UP

uNtold Stories

What are the things you dream of creating that you haven't yet made?
What ideas continue to pop up in your head that you would regret never
giving a shot?

_____

_____

_____

_____

_____

_____

_____

_____

_____

_____

_____

_____

_____

_____

_____

_____

_____

_____

_____

_____

Expressing Emotions

The beauty of creativity is that it allows you to bring forth your rich inner emotional world in a way that can be seen and shared with others. Bust out your pen or markers or paints, and make some marks in these squares that represent each emotion. There is no right or wrong answer—only expression!

Joy

Stress

love

Delight

Frustration

Hope

Happiness

Fear

Sadness

Strength

SHoeBoX of Ideas

Pretend you just found an old shoebox in the back of your closet or under your bed filled with artifacts from old ideas that you never pursued. Write them down or draw them here, and highlight the ones that are worth revisiting.

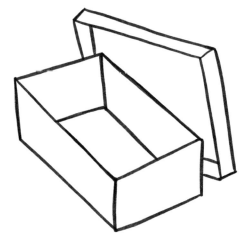

The THINGS I've MADE

As a reminder that you are in fact creative, use this page to list all the things you've made, whether in the traditional sense or otherwise. What are some of your favorite things you've made? What do you enjoy about the experience of making?

TREAT YOUR SELF-EXPRESSION like THE NECESSITY IT IS.

The art
is in the
UNFOLDING

my CReative pRoceSS

Think back to the last time you created something. Can you describe the process? How does it feel in the beginning when you're starting something new? What challenges do you encounter as you create? What do you love about the process?

SECTION 4

ConfideNCe

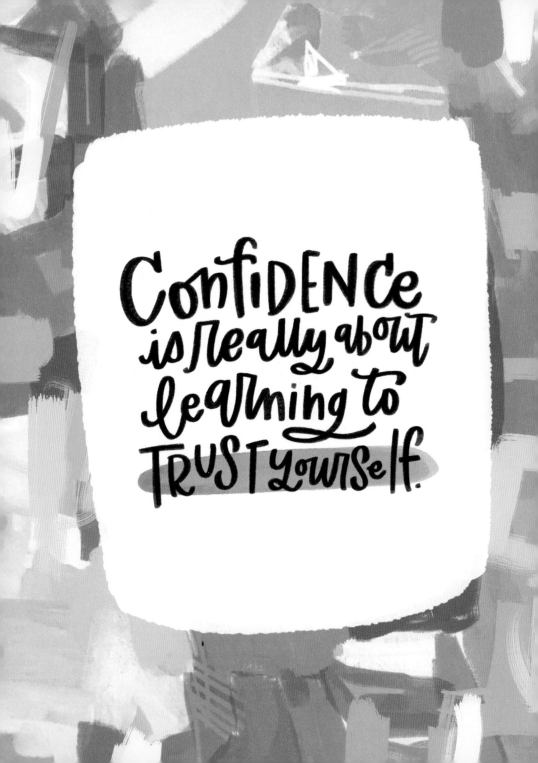

You are what you DECIDE to be.

Any spark of creativity is naturally accompanied by opposing forces of fear, self-doubt, and second-guessing. In this section, we'll address these inevitable obstacles by focusing on how to build creative confidence and how to develop a deep belief in yourself and your potential.

Confidence is not only about being able to express yourself creatively in spite of your fears of rejection. It's also about how to summon the courage to live your brightest life in all facets, even in the face of doubt and uncertainty.

I'm not an artist!

That's what I insisted five years ago when a friend caught me doodling quotes in my notebook at an event.

He had caught me in an unguarded moment and wanted to compliment me on some of my designs. Instead of graciously accepting his compliment, I immediately clarified that while yes, I "doodled" from time to time, I certainly wouldn't call myself *an artist*.

I felt too unqualified, unseasoned, and unaccomplished to call myself such a seemingly sacred word. If I said those words, it felt as if the Artist Police might emerge from a hidden corridor and slap me with a citation. *You? An artist? We're going to have to disagree with you there.*

While I had no problem with describing myself as creative, for some reason this additional label of *artist* felt way beyond me, as if it were something someone else had to decide for me and deem me worthy of.

I don't have an art degree. I don't know the "right" way to paint or draw. I'm just pretending.

These are the thoughts that were always ringing in my head, thoughts I accepted as truths for many years. I didn't have the confidence in my talent or my passion to think otherwise.

Comparing myself to others that I *did* see as artists certainly didn't help, either. Like a moth to a self-sabotaging flame, I was drawn to every "real" artist around me that looked as if they had it all together. I convinced myself that they knew something I didn't. That they *were* something I simply wasn't.

For the longest time, I let those fears and comparisons stop me from creating, and from sharing my creativity with others. I kept my writing unpublished and my doodles relegated to notebooks that collected dust.

That is, until I finally woke up to the illuminating fact that there is no Artist Tribunal waiting to call me in before a panel of judges. There is no Creativity Secret Service dressed in black suits preparing to haul me off if I declare myself an artist.

I eventually realized all I really had to do was decide it for myself.

If I started believing in my own talent, maybe that was enough. Maybe that was the key to joining this not-so-secret "secret club" that had been open to everyone this whole time.

In the beginning, the words felt so foreign coming out of my mouth: *Hi, I'm Caroline, and I'm an artist.*

But the more I said it, the more I trusted it.

We tend to think of confidence as something that is delivered to us from the outside world. If others would just give us positive feedback or validation, THEN we'll feel confident, right?

But confidence is not something that comes TO us; it comes FROM us.

We cultivate confidence through experience and practice, but it must begin with planting a seed of belief within ourselves. I started by *deciding* I was an artist, and that was the key to creating more work. Soon it snowballed and I was devoting daily time to my creativity, which in turn helped me improve my skills and boost my confidence even more.

That's not to say there weren't moments of doubt or even failure along the way. If you're out there doing something, chances are you're going to get some bruises. But the more things I created, the less pressure I put on each *individual* thing I created. A rejection didn't hurt as badly because I wasn't placing all my eggs in one basket anymore. I was creating and trying and exploring a lot of different things, and that feeling was far more positive than any one misstep was negative.

I started seeing my creative endeavors not as successes or failures, but simply as experiments. That's all life really is, anyway. Just a long list of experiments. Things we try. Assumptions we test. Experiences we learn from. Once I started to embrace that spirit of experimentation, I became less afraid of being rejected.

Confidence isn't something you have or you don't have. It's a *process*—something you move through, something you practice intentionally.

But it has to begin with you believing in yourself first. It has to start with a *decision* to ordain yourself, to recognize how capable you are and focus on things you have to offer, rather than on what you're lacking.

In the following pages, consider all that you have to offer with your gifts, creative and otherwise. Part of living your brightest life is finding your own deep source of courage. Courage to make authentic choices, show up fully as your true self, and create the things inside you that are begging to be made.

Believe in Yourself First

The ways I'm CAPable

If you want your confidence to flourish, you have to get comfortable acknowledging what you're capable of. Learn to bring your attention to your strengths, assets, gifts, and all the reasons you can succeed at what you set out to do. Use the space below to list your capabilities so you can remind yourself that the confidence you're seeking comes from a real and truthful place.

Play out THE Scenario

The fear of uncertainty often has a huge effect on our ability to show up confidently. We don't know what's going to happen, so we imagine the worst possible scenarios, and that terrifies us. To combat this uncertainty, think of the area where you most struggle with confidence. For example, it could be giving a presentation at work, or asking gallery owners to show your artwork, or having the courage to perform at an open mic night. Now imagine one of these "worst-case" scenarios that brings you anxiety (if that feels okay). Play the whole thing out to remove the uncertainty. See if writing it down removes that fear just the tiniest bit, making more room for you to find the courage to try anyway. Then write down what could go right! Play out that scenario as well and ask yourself, *Is the best-case scenario worth risking my worst-case scenario?* My bet is that it is!

think About what could go RIGHT

Draw Courage from what You KNOW to be TRUE

WHAT I know for Sure

Finding yourself in a situation where you feel the need to pretend or "fake it until you make it" can easily rattle your confidence. But while it might be your instinct to pretend in order to protect yourself against vulnerability, acknowledging the truth of the moment can be a powerful confidence builder. Think of a situation that you'd like to bring more confidence to and ask yourself, *What do you know for sure?* What truth can you anchor yourself with so you don't have that feeling of being a fraud?

the OTHER SIDE of the LeAP

What's one thing you would do in your life if you felt more confident? Instead of focusing on the fear that's holding you back from taking that leap, imagine what's waiting for you on the other side. Use the space below to explore all the possibilities that could open up to you if you found the confidence to do that thing.

FEAR is NOT the BOSS

Confidence comes from EXPERIENCE.

EXPERIENCE comes from Action.

Practice Prescription

Cultivating confidence comes from practice. The more you engage in an activity, the more you will trust in your own abilities. Fill in the blanks below to come up with a practice plan to gain experience in one area where you want to improve your confidence.

Rx ∼∼∼

To feel more CONFIDENT in my _____, I will practice this one action: _____.

I will do this ___ times a week for ___ minutes each time for the next ___ weeks.

x_____

sign here

Today I DECIDE to be...

Is there a role or part of your identity that you've been struggling to step into? Could today be the day that you decide to own it? Embody the most confident version of yourself and use the space below to write in the voice of that person you've decided to be.

Experiments, Not Failures

It's helpful to frame your experiences as experiments rather than sucesses or failures. Use the experiment results below to fill in outcomes from things that you tried but that didn't work out. Rather than letting the ones that didn't work out diminish your confidence, remind yourself what you learned from those experiments and what you'll take forward. The fact that you tried anything at all should boost your confidence!

experiment results:

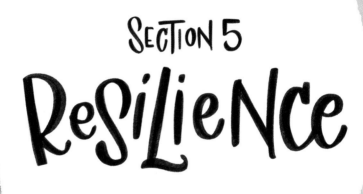

SECTION 5

RESILIENCE

You can let ADVERSITY STOP YOU or YOU can let Adversity FUEL YOU.

Learn how to LOVE the chapter you're in.

I wish I could tell you everything magically becomes easy once you start tapping in to your true core and living with authenticity. Unfortunately, that's not the case.

Living your brightest life requires you to be brave. The road to self-discovery and self-actualization is never linear; there are dips and valleys just as there are triumphs and milestones. Whether it's in the form of criticism from your family or peers, a feeling of rejection from people or institutions, or just an unexpected challenge that throws a roadblock across an otherwise great day, we all encounter bumps along the way, and resilience is a vital part of staying on the path to your brightest life.

So the question then becomes:

How can you continue to live as your brightest self even when the road gets rough?

It's important to realize that being your brightest self doesn't mean being happy all the time, pretending you're not hurt, or avoiding pain. Those emotions are a part of living a rich, complex, and full life, and staying in your authenticity means letting go of the need to pretend everything's okay all the time.

Living your brightest life is about connecting to the *fullness* of the human experience. It's about allowing yourself to feel those setbacks without letting them prevent you from showing up as your truest, fullest self in the future.

For me, that dark time came when I started my business, Made Vibrant, and things were slow to take off. I was questioning my decision, worrying every moment where my next design client was going to come from so I could pay the bills.

I started getting pounding headaches and a troublesome ache in my chest. After several visits to various doctors and ruling out cause after cause, one doctor suggested my symptoms could be anxiety-related. The thought had never even occurred to me, but it suddenly made a lot of sense.

This was the first time I'd been self-employed (rather than getting a paycheck from a company every two weeks) and I wasn't fully prepared for the emotional toll that pressure would take on me. I wanted to deliver great work, not let anyone down, and prove to myself that my dream of having a flexible, creative business was possible. But I was starting to realize that my deeply sensitive nature, combined with my overachieving tendencies (read: perfectionism), was actually a terrible fit for taking on clients.

I asked myself if the way I was operating was in alignment with who I was at my core, or if it was inhibiting me from doing things that made me feel free and joyful.

Once I was able to tap back in to my Core Compass, the solution became a lot clearer. I needed to shift my business away from client work, which allowed me to live out more of my core values—such as flexibility, control, and creativity—on a daily basis. That decision (coupled with a great therapist) helped me start to manage my anxiety, which pulled me out of that tough time.

I could have ignored the signals. I could have let the weight of that season convince me that I wasn't cut out for owning a business. But I didn't.

> I found that sense of resilience within me, which helped me *wade* through the darkness rather than run from it or be paralyzed by it.

It wasn't a particularly easy chapter of my story, but I found a way to appreciate it. It taught me that building an authentic career sometimes means making hard decisions, and it was an amazing time of growth for my relationship with my husband, Jason. Instead of judging myself for being "weak" (as we sometimes do when falsely associating sensitivity to weakness) or incapable of handling pressure, I now have so much gratitude for my sensitive nature because it allows me to feel in my body when things are out of alignment.

With a simple change in perspective, I was also able to see my anxiety issues in a positive light. Adversity brings context to triumph, just as rain gives context to sunshine. We often aren't able to fully appreciate where we've arrived without comparing it to what we went through to get there.

Another way adversity may show up is in the form of rejection, leaving you feeling as if your creative work isn't good enough. How do you stay resilient and persevere through that?

You remind yourself that rejection means you're out there *doing* something. That's one step further than most people ever get! It may not make it sting any less, but a temporarily bruised ego is a worthy price to pay for making a bold move and sharing your creativity with the world.

Allow yourself to emotionally respond to life's curveballs without self-criticism. I'm not one of those people who can just "snap out of it." The only way "out" of my emotions is *through*. So if I'm disappointed or upset, I allow myself ten minutes to feel that emotion rather than burying it. Once those ten minutes are up, I let it go. Experience it, then release it. It's the dwelling and the fuming and the replaying things over in our minds that often keeps us in a negative state.

Resilience is about engaging your power to respond to adversity in a positive way. It's about shifting your perspective to something constructive, looking for solutions, and embracing the unexpected as an adventure, not an obstacle. Sometimes, one small twist of the lens is all it takes to turn a setback into an opportunity for growth and a welcome reminder of which route is the path to your brightest life.

Lessons Learned

Write down some of the chapters of your life that have felt particularly hard or full of adversity. What lessons did those challenges teach you? Are there ways that living through those challenges made things even better on the other side?

Butterfly Effect

Think about one particularly tough period in your life and how that challenge transformed you in a lasting way. Decorate the butterfly below to represent that transformation and celebrate your resilience.

After

The transformation

before

It DOESN'T
hAve to Be
RIGHT NOW

BAdges of HoNoR

Wear your failures, rejections, or misfortunes like badges of honor. They represent things you faced and overcame. What are the experiences or opportunities that didn't go the way you wanted to, but that you can look back on and be proud of? What hard situations can you wear like badges of honor?

Peaks & Valleys

Life doesn't unfold in one linear path or smooth ride. It's full of high moments and low moments, and the lower moments help us appreciate the high moments that much more. Label the peaks and valleys of the terrain of your life with some of your triumphs and some of your low points. Then decorate and adorn the landscape of your life and relish in how rich and textured it is because it has both peaks and valleys.

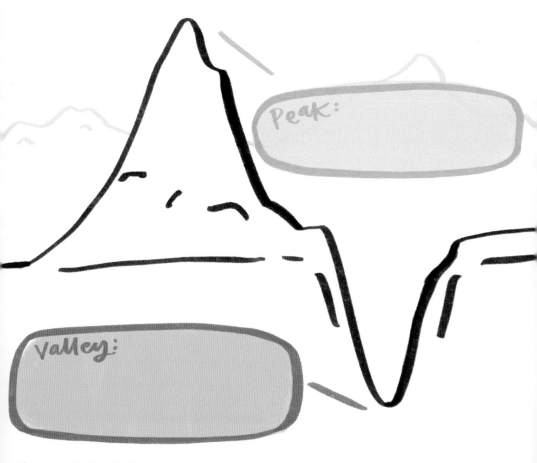

Your Resilience Mantra

Use the space provided to draw and decorate your own resilience mantra—a phrase you will mentally repeat that will give you strength to persevere when you feel like giving up.

Emergency Mood Booster

We all have days that take an unexpected bad turn and suddenly our mood is ruined. When that happens, there are intentional steps you can take to re-engage joy and lift your spirits. Treat the image below as your own personal "Break in Case of Emergency" mood-boosting kit. Add elements that are sure to lift your mood and reintroduce joy to your day.

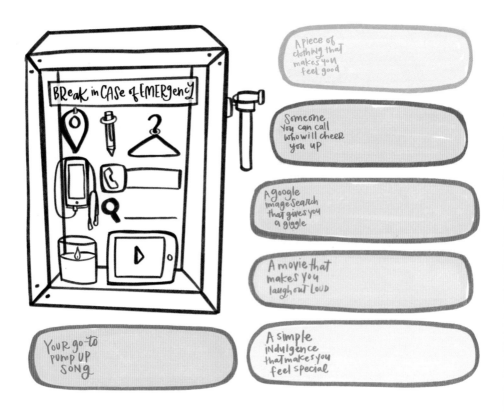

BREAK in CASE of EMERGENCY

A piece of clothing that makes you feel good

Someone you can call who will cheer you up

A google image search that gives you a giggle

A movie that makes you laugh out LOUD

Your go-to pump UP song

A simple indulgence that makes you feel special

FOCUS ONTHe Solution

Bring YOUR attention To gratitude

Thank-you Notes

When you're facing hardship, it helps to shift your perspective. One very effective way to do that is through gratitude. Use the thank-you notes below to give gratitude to the things that are *not* going well in your life, with the goal of finding the blessings or silver lining in seemingly challenging forces. How can you take a different perspective and find ways to be thankful for those things?

PROGRESS TAKES PATIENCE

Practicing Patience

When you're in the midst of feeling discouraged or dejected, it can feel as though you'll never find your way out of it, as if you'll be stuck there forever. That's when you remind yourself that you WILL make it to the other side, but progress takes patience, and patience takes *practice*. What are some ways, big and small, that you can remind yourself to be more patient? List a few situations you encounter regularly when you feel impatient, and ways that you can exercise more patience in those situations.

THE Scenic Route

Fill in your life's interstate below, including all the times unexpected challenges took you off the predictable path and into a detour that made your journey more interesting.

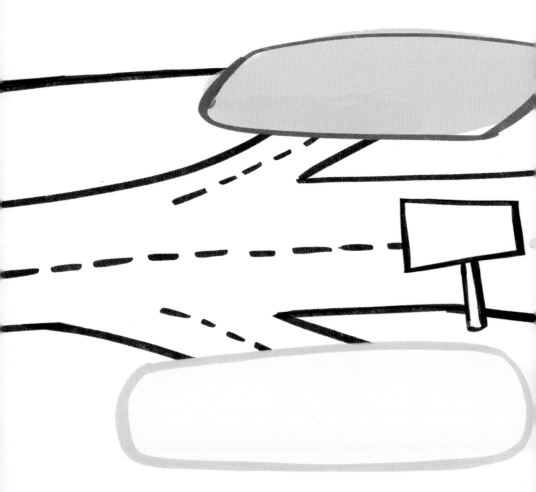

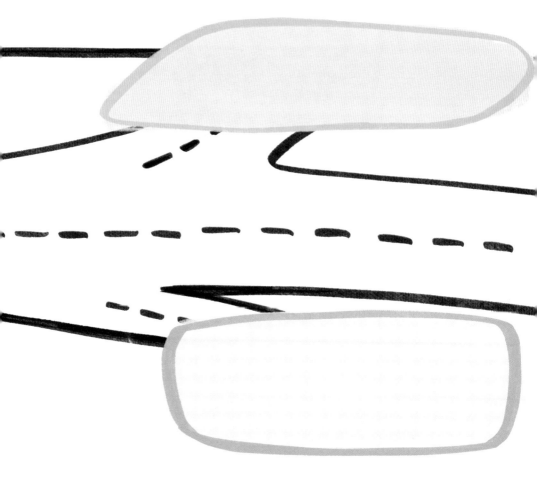

Revering Rejection

Sometimes, when someone says *No*, or *This is a bad idea*, or *You can't do it*, those interactions can completely derail us and make us doubt ourselves. But what if we flip that on its head and revere that rejection? What if instead, we celebrate the fact that a NO is getting us one step closer to a YES and let that rejection fuel us, not shut us down? That's why I want you to illustrate and decorate a phrase of rejection that someone has said to you. Allow yourself to come back to it and let it inspire you to keep reaching and prove that statement wrong.

Section 6

Intention

Everyday,
every moment,
is an opportunity
to step toward
the LIFE you
really WANT.

You control the quality of your day.

This section is all about how you design a daily life around who you are, what you care about, and what you want to create. You have the power to define what you want your days to look like, and you're the only one who can make the choices (and the trade-offs) required to make that your reality. The exercises in this section will show you how!

One of the simplest, yet most powerful, shifts in my life came when I was introduced to the concept of *intentional living*.

The idea of intention is nothing radical—it's just the simple notion that it's possible to move through your life *on purpose*.

Before I stumbled upon this idea of intention, I always viewed Life (that's *Life* with a capital L) as the one with all the power. *Life happens*, people say. It unfolds before us, comes at us, does whatever it will do TO us. Life has all the power in that scenario. It's the one in charge.

Intention, however, is about reversing that power structure. It's about changing your perspective so that life is not something that happens to you; YOU go out there and happen to life.

Intention says you have the power to mold your habits, behaviors, decisions, and reactions in such a way that *does* impact the trajectory of your life's path.

Once this became a part of my consciousness, I started to see myself as the architect of my life, not merely an inhabitant waiting for a house to be built around me. I saw that I could actually design a life around me based on all the values and core components I uncovered in my process of self-discovery.

I could decide to move to California for a life of more adventure (and sunshine)! I could choose to schedule my day so I spend time painting before opening my email. I could choose to spend less money on clothes I never wear and save up for adventurous trips to new places. I could choose to develop a daily habit of writing down my gratitude. I could choose to take a walk outside every day to reconnect with nature. These are all intentional decisions I've made in the pursuit of designing a life that supports my values.

You have the power to do this, too.

Acknowledging your own agency and taking ownership of how you experience your life is not always easy. It can be hard to take on all that responsibility ourselves. Carrying the burden of the expansive potential of our lives can be overwhelming.

To protect ourselves from this pressure, sometimes we try to share the load. We convince ourselves that other people share the responsibility for our shortcomings, our dreams deferred, our untapped potential.

We tell ourselves our ex is the reason we doubt ourselves. Or that family expectations keep us from changing careers. Or that our kids need every ounce of our time and attention, so that's why we don't make time to work on our dreams. Or that our partner feels insecure when we succeed or shine in a big way. And yes, all those things might be true.

But when we relegate the responsibility of our choices to other people, we give away our full power to create the life we dream of.

There is nothing more powerful or more motivating than finally taking ownership of your life. Every great change I've made in my life has come from the realization that I'm responsible for the way I live each day. I'm responsible for how hard I work, for how badly I want something, for whether or not I act in accordance with my core values.

Only YOU have the power to own your strengths and use them. Only YOU have the power to acknowledge your weaknesses and work on them.

Once you wake up to this power, how can you use it to form intentions that create the life you want?

First, you identify your ideal. Start by thinking about what a *great* day would look like for you. What would you be doing? How would you be feeling? Where would you go? What things would you want to work on? Who would you want to talk to?

By setting the bar for how we want each day to be, we're able to recognize when we're NOT having that ideal day and take actionable steps toward closing the gap between what's ideal and what's real.

That's when intentional choices come in to play. You *choose* what you spend your time on. You choose what you spend money on. You choose what your boundaries will be, what relationships you'll invest in, what projects you'll work on. You choose.

Living with intention is about making thoughtful redistributions of your precious resources. It's about prioritizing based on your values and what makes you feel like your brightest self.

What I want to offer you in this section is this empowering notion: You don't have to be lucky or win some long-shot lottery to experience your brightest life. You can guarantee it for yourself by defining what your brightest life means to you, working hard for it, and not settling for anything less until you get there. Gamblers accept a life of luck. Doers create a life by design.

Use the pages that follow to identify your ideal, become more aware of your own power to mold the direction of your life, and start making intentional choices about what you want that direction to be.

Recognizing Your Power

Think of the last time your day got derailed by some insignificant detail or unexpected challenge. How could you have reclaimed your power in that moment? Were there ways you could have reacted differently? Are there any areas of your life where you've been taking a passive role instead of an active role in controlling the outcome of your day or life?

More/Less List

Use the "more" space below to write down or draw things that you want to spend more time on in your life or want to do more of. Then use the "less" space to do the same for things that you want to eliminate or stop doing. Come back to the list each day until you're living out that reality and doing more of the things you love and less of the things you don't.

more

less

every day
IS A cHance
To REcommit
to YouR
VaLueS

Vibrant week recipe

I've found that the quality of my day-to-day life is greatly improved if I engage my core values on a daily basis. If I value things like stillness, creativity, and gratitude, then I can identify actions that support those values and use them as an intentional recipe for the most vibrant day and week possible. Use the table below to write in your values as ingredients to your best day, and fill in ways that you can put each one into motion on a regular basis. Then use this as a checklist to ensure each day is vibrant and in support of your brightest self!

my values	ways to incorporate into my day	M	T	W	T	F	S	S

Self-care Regimen

It can be hard for some of us to take time for ourselves—to rest or recharge or do things that just make us feel good. But we can't give to others if we're burnt out ourselves. Developing a self-care routine allows us to stay fully charged so we can live as our best selves. What are ways, big and small, that you reconnect with yourself and take care of yourself? What activities leave you feeling rejuvenated? How do you show yourself kindness on a regular basis?

Grant Your own Wishes

We often use the phrase *I wish* to talk about things we desire but don't make time for or don't act on. *I wish I could do X*, or *I wish I could find the time for Y*. The truth is, we're in control of granting our own wishes. We can choose what we spend time on and what we act on. Use the genie lamps below to write down these wishes and one action that you can take to grant them yourself, rather than waiting for the time or the permission to arrive.

where Does the time go?

We create myths for ourselves around the idea of time, that there's never enough of it to do everything we want to do. But when we take a hard look at how we spend our time, we realize that we do actually have enough, we just choose to spend it in ways that may not be aligned with the goals or values we say we have. So where does your time go? Are there activities or things that you're spending your time on that aren't in service to what you say you want or the ideal, intentional life that you've laid out for yourself? Instead of trying to do more or squeeze more in, are there things you can UNDO to make space in your day?

If you want it, make the time.

ILLUSTrate Your INTENTIONS

Visualizing new habits or intentions will help you make them a reality. Use the space below to illustrate a few new intentions for activities that will bring more vibrancy to your life. Is it to drink more water to improve your health? Draw it! Is it to spend more time with your family without technology? Illustrate that below!

Balance is a target, not a destination

reSetting the ScaleS

The concept of balance is helpful in distributing our resources effectively to the things we care about. Where in your life do you feel out of balance? How can you redistribute your time or energy to bring more balance into your life? On the right, load the scale with things that are taking up too much of your time and energy. On the left, write down some things that you could do or ways you can change your daily allotment of resources to bring things back into harmony.

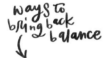

ways to bring back balance

ways I'm overdoing it

Pie IN THE Sky

Each pie below has twenty-four sections representing all the hours in the day. Fill out the first pie by labeling the amount of time that goes to work, sleep, nature, fun, family, and so on in your life now. Then fill out the second pie—your pie in the sky—with the way you want to redistribute that time more intentionally.

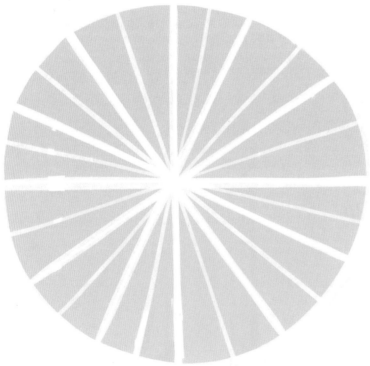

← my time Now

how I hope to
SPEND my time

SECTION 7

Self-
evolution

Let go of what WAS in order to embrace what IS.

Know when it's Time to let go.

As you move through your life, you may uncover new layers of yourself and encounter experiences that continue to mold and shape your values and beliefs. Who you think you are now is likely going to shift over time. That means a decision that feels authentic in this present moment may not feel as right one year from now. That's why it's important to be open to change.

Allow yourself to evolve and stay connected to your core self so that as new discoveries reveal themselves, you can make choices that reflect your ongoing evolution. The pages that follow will help you stay open as you continue to grow and evolve, and to be kind to yourself through that process.

Change is inevitable. You, me, the world—everything is always moving, transforming, unfolding, emerging, expanding, reacting.

The human experience is one of beautiful, relentless change.

We know this is true, yet so often we resist it. Why? Because with change comes uncertainty, discomfort, and unfamiliar territory. Times of change bring new decisions to navigate, new variables to consider, new personal challenges to confront.

But what if we embraced this progress rather than resisting it? Rather than clutching to our comfort and certainty, how much more vibrant could our lives be if we were open to the ever-changing nature of ourselves and our experience?

The beauty of this journal is that you can give yourself the tools to face whatever changes come your way, but the final piece of that puzzle is your willingness to embrace your own evolution.

My life has changed significantly many, many times over the past decade. I've quit jobs, switched careers, transferred coasts, shifted business models, and reimagined my own sense of identity more times than I can count. A designer? An artist? A writer? All three?

Each of these transformations started with a catalyst—this feeling deep within me that I was drifting out of alignment. Remember, authenticity is about aligning who you are with what you do. So when *who you are* is slowly updating (you're learning new things, rearranging priorities) while *what you do* is staying the same, that discord and distance starts to show up as pain or dissatisfaction or stress.

When you encounter that feeling, it's time to re-engage yourself as the architect of your life. It's time to lay out the blueprint once again and consider building an addition or knocking down some walls or rearranging the floor plan or even tearing the whole house down and starting over.

This is a lot easier said than done. Most often when we sense this change coming, we respond in a couple of ways. First, we fight it. Why? Because we want to hold on to the comfort of certainty. We want to stay connected to the safety of shore rather than sail out into uncharted waters. We want to wrap ourselves in the familiarity of what we know, what we feel capable of doing.

Second, we judge ourselves for even wanting to evolve. Sometimes we're in a place that we fought hard to reach. We may have had to make tough decisions and engage in difficult conversations to get where we are now, and this makes us feel unreasonable for wanting to abandon that and move toward something new. This self-judgement also stems from a fear of social judgment. *Will people think I'm erratic or flaky? Will I look unstable or lost?* Our society often values steadiness and consistency over exploration and evolution. But living your brightest life is about rejecting that conventional frame and leaning in to a more authentic way of being, one that embraces evolution.

In times of change, remind yourself that you are *allowed* to evolve. Do not beat yourself up over making a different decision now than you did last year or even last month. Our sense of self can be a moving target. Keep checking back in to make sure you're aiming at the right thing with your decisions and goals.

When you feel that discord bubbling up again and you're on the cusp of a transformation, trust the flow of things and honor what you're feeling. Tap back into that Core Compass of yours and follow where it's leading you.

This will require that you let go of things, which is never easy, but it's necessary. To get closer to a truer way of being, there are things that represent a part of who you *were* but not who you *are* now that will need to be released. This could be a relationship that has to end, a routine that's no longer serving you, or a project that has run its course.

When I encounter a season of life that feels particularly hard, it's usually because I'm trying to hold on to something the deeper part of me has already outgrown; I'm trying to keep my actions and behaviors static, while my true self is barreling forward to a new way of being.

The longer you hold on to what's not serving your true self, the longer you postpone the joy of living your brightest life.

In this process of evolution, remember that you will never arrive at a final destination. You won't wake up one day to find that the journey is complete and you've reached the summit of the self-actualization mountain.

Instead, the journey IS the destination. The process never ends. The more you can get comfortable with that, the more you can find pleasure in the endless cycle of self-discovery, and the more satisfaction, contentment, and joy will open up to you.

Come back to this section every time you sense yourself approaching a period of change. Remind yourself that updating your life to match your ever-evolving self is all part of the process.

Change is uncomfortable, but not as uncomfortable as missing out on your brightest life.

I HAD a dream...

Part of allowing yourself to evolve is acknowledging that what you want now might not be what you wanted then. How have your dreams changed and evolved over time? What shifted within you that made you realize a desire you once had no longer feels true?

THE Times are a-changin'

Much like how technology keeps evolving and changing as time goes on (hello, chunky '90s cell phone), we are constantly changing and evolving. Use the illustrations below as your own evolutionary timeline, and label each point with how you've seen your inner self change and upgrade and grow from childhood to a young adulthood to now.

Break-up letter

An essential part of moving on is letting go, so use this space to write your own Dear John letter to break up with one thing in your life you're ready to move on from. *Dear story about how I'm not good enough, it's time to say goodbye. Dear old job, I'm ready to pursue something new. Dear toxic friendship, you're not doing me any favors.*

Dear _____,

appreciate how far you've come

Acknowledging Progress

So often we're improving or evolving in such tiny increments, that it can feel as if we're standing still. It's not until we finally take a moment to stop and step back that we can see all those inches stacked end to end. That's why it's important to zoom out and acknowledge our progress over time. In what ways have you grown or improved in the past year? What new skills have you acquired? What things have you learned about yourself that you hope to carry forth into the next season of your life?

UNPack your Bags

We all have baggage that weighs us down and holds us back. It could be experiences that burned us, or failures that still sting, or fears we keep inside. Time to unpack that baggage and bring it out into the light. What do you have packed away inside that you can unpack and let go of? Draw and label it below so you can finally feel lighter!

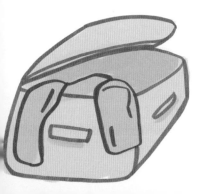

Come Back To THE Now

One technique for embracing change, rather than clutching tightly to the past, is to simply live in this moment, to lean into whatever circumstances or feelings you're having NOW, without attaching judgment. How do you remind yourself to come back to the present moment? Are there strategies you use to remind yourself to stay in the here and now so you can take this day, this moment, as it arrives?

FIND PEACE IN the PRESENT

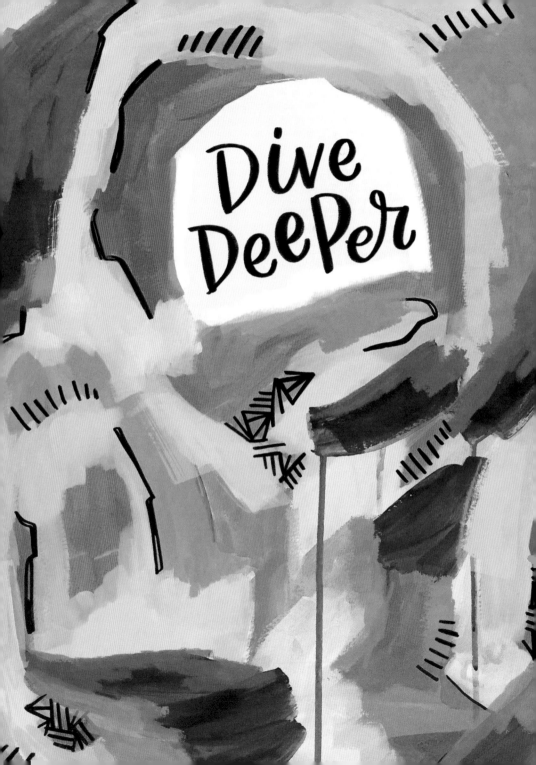

Reconnecting to your Core

Tapping in to your brightest core self is an ongoing endeavor. Remember to reconnect with yourself to make sure you're living in alignment with your ever-changing core. What are some ways that you plan to continue to reconnect with your true inner self in the future? Can you mark a date on your calendar to come back to this journal, or is there a date you can make a "Reconnection Day" holiday? What are your strategies for staying connected to yourself as you change and evolve?

BE
Kind
to
yourself

Left turn Ahead

You know that gut feeling you get when you're getting ready to embark
on a new season of life? What signals tell you it's time to recalibrate and
reevaluate your decisions? What are some signs that indicate to you that
process is coming? Label the road signs below with the different ways
your gut tells you it's time to take a left turn and shake things up.

FReSH Start

To ease the discomfort that often comes with a season of change, it helps to embrace the excitement of new circumstances. What are ways that you can embrace that feeling of starting fresh? What changes can you make to your immediate environment, your routines, or your mindsets, that will help you feel renewed, rather than uncertain in a new period of your evolution?

Trust
THE
Flow
OF
Things

THE
Journey
IS the
Destination

And the journey continues...

I hope the words and exercises in these pages have helped you uncover insights about who you are at the deepest level, and I hope the lessons I've shared with you will continue to lead you to a life that supports the truest, best version of who you are. Remember, this journey never ends. Come back to these pages whenever you need to tap back into that bright ball of pure potential within you.

I believe the world is a better, more beautiful place when we're all living our brightest lives.

Now get out there and start living yours!